ARCO-AIRCAM AVIATION SERIES

No. 33

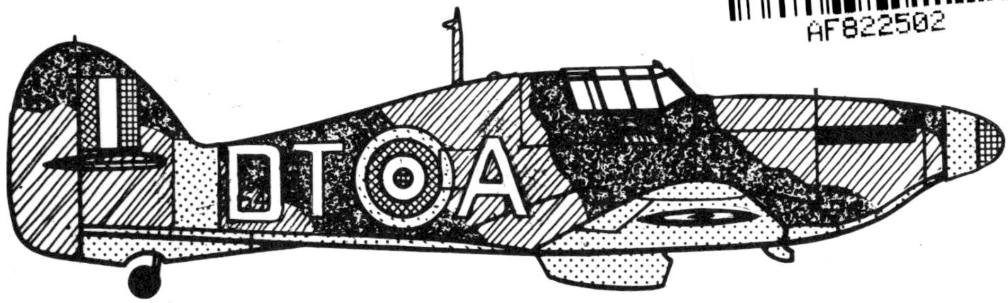

Mk. I, No. 257 "Burma" Squadron, Coltishall, November – December 1940, Battle of Britain. Flown by Sqdn. Ldr. R. R. Stanford-Tuck. This side-view shows the starboard side pattern of Scheme B. (Right) The Burmese flag insignia carried on the starboard side under the cockpit. Colours are: Red flag with Union Jack with a peacock in natural colours on a white disc. BURMA in white on camouflage. The port side carried a row of 26 Swastikas under the cockpit.

HAWKER HURRICANE MK.I/IV
IN ROYAL AIR FORCE & FOREIGN SERVICE

Compiled and Illustrated by Richard Ward

Text by Christopher F. Shores

ACKNOWLEDGEMENTS
The Hurricane: first of the eight-gun fighters, mainstay of Fighter Command during the Battle of Britain. No other fighter fought on more fronts for so long—1939–1945, was more adaptable to the changing tactical requirements of the War years nor able to absorb battle damage better than the Hurricane.
My thanks to all those who assisted with photographs and information whose names are listed below in alphabetical order:
Charles E. Brown, Hawker Aircraft, Imperial War Museum, Francis K. Mason, E. Ritaranta, Christopher F. Shores, G. J. R. Skillen, Lt.-Col. M. C. Terlinden, R. Ward.

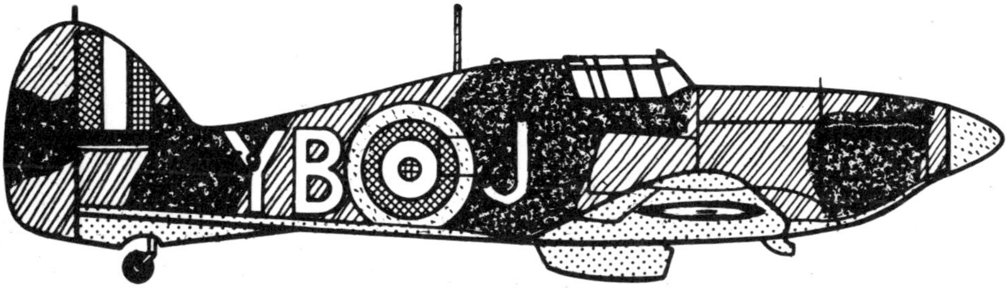

Mk. I, No. 17 Squadron, Debden, September 1940, Battle of Britain. This side-view shows the starboard side pattern of Scheme A. (Right) Personal insignia on port side only. Colours are: Pink face and arm, blue jumper, white cap, wings and trousers, black trim.

PUBLISHED BY

Arco Publishing Company, Inc., 219 Park Avenue South, New York, N.Y. 10003

First Published by Osprey Publishing Ltd. and Printed in Great Britain

Library of Congress No. 75-113960 · SBN 668-02316-3

Three good detail photographs of the Hurricane prototype in original configuration. (Hawker)

Neat formation by Hurricane Mk. I's of No. 85 Squadron towards the end of the Battle of Britain. Note the white hexagon under the cockpit and the variation in the underwing roundel size. (IWM)

HAWKER HURRICANE

In January 1934 Hawker Aircraft began design work on a new private venture monoplane fighter incorporating the latest Rolls-Royce PV-12 engine—soon to be known as the Merlin. Impressed by the first design, the Air Ministry wrote specification F 36/34 around Hawker's project; initially it was proposed to arm the aircraft with four .303 in. Vickers machine guns, two alongside the engine and one in each wing, but availability of the far superior Browning gun of the same calibre led to a change, and when the prototype first flew on 6 November 1935 it had provision for no less than eight of these guns in batteries of four in each wing. Powered by a 900 h.p. Merlin "C", which drove a two-blade wooden airscrew, the new aircraft reached a top speed of 315 m.p.h. at 16,200 feet—a performance well in advance of that being achieved by immediate contemporaries abroad, such as the Messerschmitt Bf 109V-1 and Heinkel He 112V-1 in Germany, the Morane 405 in France and the Curtiss Hawk 75 and Seversky 2XP in the United States.

After tests Hawker prepared to produce 1,000 examples of the fighter in anticipation of orders, and on 3 June 1936 came the first of these for 600 aircraft for the R.A.F., the name Hurricane being approved at the same time. The first production aircraft, with a Merlin II engine of 1,030 h.p., flew on 12 October 1937, and deliveries commenced at once. These initial aircraft reached 318 m.p.h. at 17,400 feet and climbed at a rate of 2,450 feet per minute, but they also featured fabric-covered wings, and lacked pilot armour and bullet-proof windscreens.

Despite the R.A.F.'s urgent need for fighters, export orders were permitted and a number were sold from the first production batch, licences also being given for the manufacture of the aircraft in Belgium and Yugoslavia. Meanwhile development continued, and it was soon discovered that a three-blade de Havilland or Rotol airscrew gave a somewhat better performance, offering a maximum speed of 324 m.p.h.; future orders were modified to incorporate one or other of these, and fighters already in service were retrospectively brought up to this standard. On 28 April 1939 the first metal-covered wings were tested, and deliveries of aircraft fitted with these commenced in September 1939. To increase production, Gloster Aircraft Co. also began a Hurricane production line, the first aircraft being delivered during October 1939; 1,924 Mark Is were to be built by Hawkers and 1,850 by Glosters. After 20 examples had been delivered to Canada, the Canadian Car and Foundry Co. also set up production, their first Hurricane being rolled out in June 1940.

Early combat experience in France showed the need for better protection, and modification in 1940 included the fitting of pilot armour and bullet-proof windscreens. First tests with 20 mm. armament were made during February 1940, and by the summer a few aircraft had been equipped with these guns for service operational trials. More engine power also became available and in June 1940 the first Mark II with a Merlin XX of 1,280 h.p. flew; the production version, the Mark IIA Series 1, was in other ways similar to the Mark I, but the increased power offered an improved top speed of 342 m.p.h. at 22,000 feet; this version began entering service with the R.A.F. in September 1940, followed a month later by the Series 2, which featured a slightly lengthened and strengthened fuselage. These versions were basically interim aircraft, and were followed by the Mark IIB and C; the B version was armed with twelve .303 in. machine guns and the C with four 20 mm. Hispano cannons; in both cases the wings had been strengthened to allow a pair of 250 lb. or 500 lb. bombs to be carried. Neither version entered service until well into 1941.

In September 1941 a further version flew, the Mark IID, fitted initially with a pair of underwing Rolls-Royce BF 40 mm. anti-tank cannons with 17 rounds per gun; main production aircraft of this type carried Vickers "S" guns of the same calibre with 15 rounds each, and entered service during 1942. A pair of wing-mounted .303s were retained to fire tracer for aiming purposes.

Production in Canada continued, but from mid-1941 onwards Merlins built under licence by Packard in the U.S. were fitted; and after production of the Mark IIA ceased, all further variants were given special Mark numbers, beginning with the X—similar to the R.A.F. Mark IIB. This version was also fitted with a Hamilton Standard propeller, and many of those used by the R.C.A.F. were not fitted with spinners as this airscrew featured an acceptable streamlined boss. The Mark XI was built entirely for the R.C.A.F., and this was followed by the principal production version, the Mark XII.

In the U.K. development continued with the Mark IIE, which was fitted with a universal wing which could carry 40 mm. guns, drop tanks, bombs or rocket projectiles—the first tests by Hurricanes with these latter weapons being undertaken in February 1942. After 270 Mark IIEs had been produced, the designation was changed to Mark IV (the Mark III was a projected Packard-Merlin powered version which was not built); powered by a 1,620 h.p. Merlin 24 or 27, the Mark IV when carrying eight 60 lb. rockets reached a maximum speed of 284 m.p.h. at 13,500 feet. Five hundred and twenty-four Mark IVs were built, and two of these fitted with Merlin 32 engines and four-blade airscrews as Mark Vs, but this version was not ordered into production.

The last aircraft to be built, a Mark IIC, was completed in September 1944, by which time production totalled 14,233 aircraft (including Sea Hurricanes, of which more later), 10,030 built by Hawkers, 2,750 by Glosters and 1,451 by the Canadian Car and Foundry Co., together with two by Avions Fairey in Belgium. A further uncertain number (not exceeding 20) were produced in Yugoslavia.

The Hurricane in British Commonwealth Service

The first squadron of the R.A.F. to receive Hurricanes was No. 3 at Northolt, this unit taking over the services's first monoplane fighter during December 1937. In March 1938 3 Squadron followed suite, though in July it re-converted to Gladiator biplanes; in April 56 Squadron received the new aircraft and by the end of the year ten squadrons were Hurricane-equipped: Nos. 1, 32, 43, 56, 73, 79, 85, 87, 111 and 151.

During the year seven Hurricanes were sent to South Africa, where they formed part of 1 S.A.A.F. Squadron, flying alongside Hawker Fury biplanes. Production proceeded apace during 1939, and in March 501 "County of Gloucester" Squadron became the first Auxiliary unit to receive the new fighters; both 504 "County of Nottinghamshire" and 605 "County of Warwick" Squadrons also took deliveries of Hurricanes before the outbreak of war. Despite the fulfilment of several foreign orders, 467 Hurricanes had been delivered to the R.A.F. by the time war broke out on 3 September 1939, and 17 squadrons were fully equipped; 3 Squadron had again converted during May, and was joined by 17, 46 and 213 Squadrons.

Immediately hostilities commenced, four Hurricane squadrons were sent to Europe; and 1 and 73 Squadrons moved to Central France as part of the Advanced Air Striking Force, to provide escort and airfield defence to the R.A.F.'s Battle and Blenheim squadrons which were making reconnaissance and bombing raids over German territory. Nos. 85 and 87 Squadrons accompanied two Gladiator squadrons, 607 and 615, as part of the Air Component, based in North-Western France near the Belgian border to provide air cover for the British Expeditionary Force in the line.

Efforts continued to increase the number of Hurricane squadrons available, and by the end of April 1940 six more squadrons had converted to, or been formed on these aircraft, these being 145, 229, 242, 245, 253 and 601 Squadrons. Meanwhile, in France 615 Squadron was in the midst of converting from its Gladiators, and 607 Squadron was to start doing so the next month.

Over France the Hurricane had already seen some action, the units of the A.A.S.F. being mainly involved; on 30 October 1939 Pilot Officer P. W. O. Mould of 1

Two line-ups of Hurricane Mk. I's of No. 111 Squadron at Northolt. No. 111 was the first squadron to be equipped with the Hurricane, the first aircraft arriving in late 1937. (Hawker)

Squadron made the first Hurricane claim when he shot down a Dornier 17, and by early May 1940 Flying Officer E. J. "Cobber" Kain of 73 Squadron had already claimed five aircraft destroyed, to become the first R.A.F. "ace" of World War II. In Britain several units had had brushes with various intruders, mainly reconnaissance aircraft off the coast, and several of these had been shot down.

On the morning of 10 May 1940 the German offensive against France and the Low Countries began, and at once all the R.A.F.'s fighter squadrons on the Continent were heavily involved trying to stop the advancing columns; the units of the Air Component covered the B.E.F. in its initial dash into Belgium. Further squadrons were at once flown over, 3, 79 and 504 Squadrons joining the Component, while 501 joined the A.A.S.F.; and three days later 32 more aircraft were sent, this time in half-squadrons. The fighting for the units of the Component was particularly desperate as the B.E.F. was forced back to the Dunkirk area, and by 21 May all were ordered to return to England. During the fighting these units had claimed well over 250 victories for the loss of about 22 in air combat, but altogether 75 Hurricanes were destroyed by enemy action, many on the ground; 120 unserviceable aircraft were burnt to avoid capture, and only 66 returned to home establishment.

Over the next week squadrons were thrown into battle over the Channel and the Dunkirk area as the B.E.F. was evacuated, the Hurricanes now being joined by Fighter Command's other types, the Spitfires and Defiants. Hurricane units seeing action in this fighting included Nos. 32, 79, 213, 242, 245 and 605 Squadrons. The A.A.S.F. squadrons remained in France, withdrawing on 3 June to the south-west of Paris, and covering French forces and the remaining British troops who were making for the Atlantic ports. Joined at this time by 17 and 242 Squadrons, the A.A.S.F. continued to fight until withdrawn via the Channel Islands, by which time the five squadrons had lost 66 aircraft to all causes; 1 Squadron had been particularly successful, claiming some 155 victories, but all units were in dire need of rest and re-equipment.

While this action had been going on, 46 Squadron with Hurricanes had been sent to Norway where a German invasion had taken place, and arrived off the coast on the carrier H.M.S. *Glorious* on 26 May. Three aircraft were flown off and arrived at the allotted base at Skaanland, but nosed over on landing due to the state of the runway; the other 15 were diverted to Bardufoss. Here they put up a splendid performance under very poor conditions until 7 June, when the pilots were ordered to destroy their aircraft and evacuate. Rather than do so, volunteers flew the surviving serviceable Hurricanes to successful deck-landings on *Glorious*; but this daring exploit was brought to nought when the carrier was later intercepted and sunk by the *Scharnhorst* and *Gneisnau*, all the Hurricanes and most of the pilots being lost.

The battle for Britain now began, and during July many Hurricane units were involved in fights over shipping in the Channel. When the attack was turned on England itself early in August, 2,309 Hurricanes had been delivered; 26 squadrons of these aircraft were operational, three were partly operational and four were in the process of re-equipping. The story of the Battle of Britain is well known and has been adequately covered elsewhere, but suffice it to say that it was the Hurricane units, forming the main bulk of Fighter Command, which took the greatest weight of the attack, claimed the majority of the victories, and suffered the heaviest losses. Prior to the summer of 1940, 242 Squadron had been composed mainly of Canadian personnel, but during the Battle of Britain the first R.C.A.F. fighter unit to reach England began operations, this being 1 R.C.A.F. Squadron (later re-numbered 401 Squadron to avoid confusion). Additionally, after the fall of France many pilots from Occupied Europe had reached England, at first serving in R.A.F. squadrons; national squadrons were then formed, 302 and 303 (Polish) Squadrons and 310 (Czech) Squadron all seeing action before the end of the Battle. By late autumn six such squadrons had been formed, four

Hurricane Mk. I showing the starboard side of scheme "A" camouflage pattern. (Hawker)

Polish and two Czech, and in November, 71 "Eagle" Squadron began forming with American volunteer pilots. At the close of 1940 the number of Hurricane squadrons in the U.K. had risen to 43; late in the year, as the *Luftwaffe* turned to night bombing, several of these, 85, 96 and 151 included, turned to night fighting, and early in the New Year began supplementing their Hurricanes with Defiants for this purpose.

When war with Italy broke out in the Middle East in June 1940, there was just one Hurricane available to the R.A.F. in this theatre. Before the fall of France a number were flown out across that country, and these soon formed a flight of 80 Squadron. As more became available, 274 Squadron was formed in August with one flight from 80 Squadron and one from 33, as the first all-Hurricane unit in the Middle East. Apart from the odd interception of Savoia SM 79 bombers, the Hurricanes saw little action over the Egyptian and Libyan Deserts until the first Libyan Campaign began in early December. Meanwhile, however, 418 Flight was sent from the U.K. aboard H.M.S. *Argus*, flying off 12 Hurricanes to Malta to join with the few Gladiators on hand there and form 261 Squadron for the island's defence. These early arrivals in the Mediterranean area were fitted with "pigeon-chested" Vokes intakes to filter out the dust and sand, and these created additional drag, reducing top speed to 312 m.p.h.

By December, when the successful British drive across Libya began, 33 and 274 Squadrons were fully operational on Hurricanes, and the first aircraft of 73 Squadron from England had arrived, having flown right across the continent from West Africa, where they had been delivered by carrier. In January the first German aircraft appeared in the Mediterranean, operating initially over Malta where 261 Squadron was hotly engaged throughout the first quarter of 1941. The advance in the Desert had reached its limit by February and in that month Hurricanes were sent to partly re-equip 80 Squadron, which had been sent to Greece late in 1940 equipped with Gladiators; the following month 33 Squadron joined the former unit here. Late in March the German *Afrika Korps*, newly-arrived in Libya, attacked the British forces there and sent them reeling back into Egypt; 274 Squadron had been withdrawn to rest, so only 73 and 3 R.A.A.F. Squadrons, the latter recently re-equipped with Hurricanes, plus a few tactical reconnaissance Hurricanes in 6 Squadron, faced the onslaught of the Axis, now covered by Messerschmitt Bf 109Es of I/JG 27 and Bf 110Cs of III/ZG 26.

Early in April the Germans attacked Greece, and despite a gallant defence the Allied forces were quickly driven out; it was at this time that Sqn./Ldr. M. T. Pattle, commanding officer of 33 Squadron, built up what was probably the highest score obtained by any R.A.F. pilot in the Second World War. Commonwealth forces withdrew to Crete, where they were attacked in early May by paratroops and other forces. A tiny handful of Hurricanes flown by pilots of 33, 80, 112 and 805 (F.A.A.) Squadrons fought until all were destroyed, such cover as was possible then being given by long-range Hurricanes of 274 Squadron from Egypt.

On the brighter side, three S.A.A.F. squadrons operated Hurricanes in East Africa during this period, gaining complete mastery over the *Regia Aeronautica* while supporting a successful campaign on the ground. No. 2 S.A.A.F. Squadron, with Hurricanes, Gladiators and Furies, operated in the south over Ethiopia, joined later by

Hurricane Mk. I's of No. 85 Squadron on Merville airfield during the German offensive in the Low Countries. (IWM)

the all-Hurricane 3 S.A.A.F. Squadron. To the north, 1 S.A.A.F. Squadron flew over Eritrea, initially with Gladiators, but from December 1940 with increasing numbers of Hurricanes. By early April the whole of Eritrea, and Addis Ababa, the capital of Ethiopia, were in Allied hands, and no further serious aerial opposition was met before the final surrender of the remaining Italian forces later in the year.

In England early in 1941 the first Hurricane IIBs were entering service with 601 and 605 Squadrons, and the first IICs with 1 and 3 Squadrons, and units now took part in the early offensive sweeps over Occupied Europe, also carrying out strafing missions with small formations of fighters. More new squadrons were formed during the year; these including 81, 121 (Eagle), 133 (Eagle), 134, 135, 136, 255, 256, 260, 315 (Polish), 317 (Polish), 331 (Norwegian) and 402 (R.C.A.F.) Squadrons. The day of the Hurricane as a pure fighter in Western Europe was nearing an end, however, and by the close of the year 71, 81, 111, 121, 133, 145, 302, 303, 306, 308, 310, 312, 315, 316, 317, 331, 401, 501 and 504 Squadrons had converted to Spitfires, 56 Squadron to Typhoons, 601 Squadron to Airacobras, and 85, 96, 225 and 256 Squadrons to various night-fighting types such as Defiants and Beaufighters.

Following the German attack on Russia in June 1941, an R.A.F. Wing—No. 151, composed of 81 and 134 Squadrons with Hurricane IIA and IIB fighters—went to North Russia in August to introduce the Hurricane, flying a short period of successful operations. The pilots of this Wing claimed 16 victories for only one loss, before handing the aircraft to the 72nd Regiment of the Soviet Naval Air Fleet, and returning to Britain.

Reinforcement of the Middle East continued apace in 1941; during the spring and early summer 213, 229 and 238 Squadrons arrived in Egypt, though at first they were not in sufficient strength to operate as full squadrons, and were attached to existing units. A second Hurricane unit, 185 Squadron, was formed on Malta; but in the summer, after a most noteworthy defence of the island, a very tired 261 Squadron was disbanded. 46 Squadron's aircraft, on the way to Egypt, were retained on the island with their pilots, forming the nucleus of 126 Squadron, and at the same time 249 Squadron arrived from England also.

While the British forces had been in trouble in Greece and the Desert, the Iraqis had taken the opportunity to stage a pro-Axis coup, but hostilities against the R.A.F. bases there were quickly dealt with; Hurricanes of 94 Squadron, which moved in from Aden, took part in the latter stages of the fighting. In Egypt, after the return from Greece, 30 Squadron (previously a Blenheim IF unit) was re-equipped with Hurricanes, and 33 and 80 Squadrons were brought up to strength. Immediately following the Iraqi operations, Allied forces invaded Vichy French Syria, 80 Squadron taking part from the start, joined during the campaign by pilots and aircraft of 260 Squadron, newly-arrived from Britain, and by a composite Hurricane/Gladiator unit formed temporarily for the campaign as 127 Squadron. Naval pilots of 806 Squadron also operated ex-R.A.F. Hurricanes on patrol duties at this time. After the end of the fighting 127 Squadron was disbanded, then forming the nucleus of a new 261 Squadron which provided cover to Allied forces occupying Iran.

Following the conclusion of the main fighting in East Africa, 1 and 2 S.A.A.F. Squadrons moved up to this area, where the latter then re-equipped with Tomahawks; 3 R.A.A.F. Squadron had also converted to these aircraft in the meantime. A new Hurricane squadron formed during this period was 450 (R.A.A.F.) Squadron, and three Tactical Reconnaissance units, 208, 237 (Rhodesian) and 451 (R.A.A.F.), all received these aircraft also. By the opening of the big "Crusader" offensive in mid-November the Western Desert Air Force disposed some dozen squadrons of Hurricanes, including 30, 33, 80, 94, 208, 229, 237, 238, 260, 274, 451 and 1 S.A.A.F., together with the personnel of 803 and 806 Squadrons, F.A.A., who formed part of the Royal Naval Fighter Squadron which flew Hurricanes alongside the R.A.F. from land bases in the Desert.

By the end of 1941 the Hurricane was well past its best; in Western Europe it was operated mainly as a fighter-bomber against shipping and coastal targets, and for night intruding operations (1 and 3 Squadrons gaining considerable successes in the latter rôle), the first fighter-bomber sorties having been flown in October. In the Desert the first such missions were undertaken by 80 Squadron during November, but in this latter area Hurricanes were now suffering increasingly severe losses to the newly-arrived Bf 109Fs of the *Luftwaffe*. On Malta, too, as the second great German assault on the island began in December, the Hurricanes found their job ever more difficult, even when joined by aircraft and personnel from parts of 242 and 605 Squadrons.

At this moment the Japanese struck in the Far East, where in December 1941 no Hurricanes were based at all. Fortunately, a number of squadrons were under way to the Middle East and these were diverted to the new area. A group of pilots from 17, 135, 136 and 232 Squadrons reached Singapore in mid-January 1942 and formed a composite squadron under 232's mantle, bearing the initial weight of the assault on this island. Later in the month the main bulk of 232 Squadron, accompanied by 258 Squadron, flew off the carrier H.M.S. *Indomitable* to the East Indies, and these units moved forward to defend Singapore and Sumatra until the fall of both islands. In Java the squadrons were joined by those parts of 242 and 605 Squadrons which had not reached Malta, but attrition caused a contraction of units into each other until only 242 Squadron remained. Fighting alongside Dutch and American fighters, the Hurricanes claimed many more of the enemy than they lost themselves, but the ground situation was against them, and on 8 March 1942 all resistance on Java came to an end.

Meanwhile, in Burma 17 Squadron arrived from India in January, joining Buffaloes and A.V.G. Tomahawks for the defence of Rangoon. No. 135 Squadron followed, and these two units fought throughout the retreat into India, putting up a very effective defence until most of their aircraft were destroyed on the ground. In March *Indomitable* rushed 30 and 261 Squadrons to Ceylon from the Middle East, and here pilots evacuated from Java formed a new 258 Squadron; on 5 and 9 April 1942 these units and R.N. Fulmar squadrons defended the island against attacks launched by Admiral Nagumo's superb carrier striking force, exacting a heavy toll of the attackers, but suffering substantial losses themselves.

At home during 1942 many more squadrons converted to Spitfires and Typhoons, and while new units were frequently formed on Hurricanes, they rarely saw any action before exchanging them for more modern types. The exception to this was in regard to the specialized types, 184 Squadron being formed with the first Hurricane IIDs

Above, both pictures: An untidy formation by Hurricane Mk. I's of No. 73 Squadron, No. 67 Wing, Advanced Air Striking Force, flying over France in bumpy conditions. Both squadrons of No. 67 Wing deleted their code letters but E is still flying with the full code, note the red, white and blue rudder stripes applied for the benefit of French fighters. (IWM)

Right: Hurricane Mk. I's of No. 1 Squadron coming in to land at Vassingcourt, France, in September 1939. (IWM)

The Langley Airfield defence Hurricane Mk. IIa. It was intended that should Langley be attacked by lone raiders the Hurricane, piloted by any Hawker or RAF pilot who might be available, should take-off to intercept. The aircraft was permanently maintained with full tanks and loaded guns but there is no record to show it was ever flown into action. Left, close-up of the nose insignia. (Hawker)

late in 1941.

In the Middle East the first Spitfires began arriving in March 1942, going initially to Malta, where 249 Squadron, followed by 126 and then 185 Squadrons re-equipped. No. 229 Squadron moved to the island in the spring, but was disbanded after heavy losses, and apart from a few fighter-bombers Hurricanes had ceased to operate from the island by the summer. In the Desert several squadrons converted to Kittyhawks, including 94, 260 and 450 Squadrons, but others soldiered on until the Alamein battle in October, and were joined by new units. These were 127 (re-formed) and 335 (the first Greek fighter squadron) for fighting duties, 40 S.A.A.F. Squadron for tactical reconnaissance, and 7 S.A.A.F. Squadron, which after a disastrous period as a fighter-bomber unit joined 6 Squadron, R.A.F., in equipping with Hurricane IID "tank-busters". Units which took part in Montgomery's autumn offensive were 33, 80, 127, 213, 238, 274, 335 and 1 S.A.A.F. Squadrons, operating as fighter-bombers and providing defence against Stuka attacks on the forward troops; 73 Squadron, flying night strafing attacks, 208 and 40 S.A.A.F. Squadrons, carrying out tactical reconnaissance missions; and 94 and 417 (R.C.A.F.) Squadrons (94 having re-converted to Hurricanes), providing rear area defence.

After the breakthrough at Alamein 213 and 238 Squadrons moved ahead to operate from a landing ground deep in the Desert behind enemy lines, harassing retreating columns; but apart from this none of the Hurricane day fighter units moved forward, only 73 for night work and 40 S.A.A.F. Squadron for reconnaissance, moving up to Tripoli.

From England, Hurricane units flew fighter-bomber support missions during the Dieppe operation on 19 August 1942, and on 8 November squadrons transferred from England supported Allied landings in Algeria as part of Operation "Torch". No. 43 Squadron, with Hurricane IICs, was the first R.A.F. unit to land in this part of Africa, and it was soon followed by 32, 87 and 253 Squadrons for fighting duties, as well as 225 and 241 Squadrons for army co-operation, in company with a large number of Spitfire squadrons. After initial operations the Hurricanes were retained for convoy patrols and defence of base areas, and units began to receive Spitfires as replacements as quickly as these became available.

To the east, 1 S.A.A.F. Squadron with the W.D.A.F. had converted to Spitfires late in 1942, and by the Mareth Line battle in March 1943 only 6 Squadron (again with Mark IID "tank-busters") and 73 Squadron were operating over the front, 40 S.A.A.F. Squadron being in the midst of re-equipping with Spitfires for its tactical reconnaissance duties. By the fall of the Axis in Africa in May, 43 and 225 Squadrons had also converted to Spitfires, and 32, 87 and 253 Squadrons had all received at least one of these aircraft.

No. 73 Squadron, flying at night, was the only Hurricane unit to participate in the Allied landings on Sicily in mid-1943. No. 6 Squadron was converting to Hurricane IVs, and all other Hurricane units in the Middle East were on patrol duties, based along the whole length of the North African coast. These included 32, 33, 74 (newly arrived from England), 87, 94, 123, 127, 134, 173, 208, 213, 237, 238, 241, 253, 274, 335, 451, 3 S.A.A.F. (recently arrived from East Africa) and 7 S.A.A.F. Squadron. A second Greek squadron, 336, was working-up on Hurricanes at this time. Many of these units were also operating a few Spitfires, and by the end of 1943, 32, 33, 73, 74, 80, 87, 123, 127, 237, 238, 253, 274, 336, 451 and 3 S.A.A.F. Squadrons had all converted to Spitfires, and 134 Squadron had moved to the Far East.

Meanwhile, in the Far East, the Hurricane had become the backbone of the R.A.F. in India. By late 1942 there were 13 squadrons of these aircraft there and in Ceylon, including 17, 30, 67, 79, 135, 146, 258, 273, 261, 607, 615, and 681, the latter being a P.R. unit (ex-3 P.R.U.). Late in the year the Japanese began a series of attacks on Calcutta; 17 and 79 Squadrons operated from Red Road, a highway in the city, against these raids, and 67 and 607 Squadrons also took part in this fighting. Early in 1943 the first Allied offensive into Burma was launched, supported by 261, 615 and newly re-equipped 28 Squadron. This offensive, a drive down the Mayun peninsula, was pushed back into India by the end of May.

Considerable air fighting continued over Northern Burma and the Indian frontier during the early months of 1943, and by June three Blenheim squadrons, 11, 20 and 60, had been re-equipped with Hurricanes, mainly for ground attack duties. This pattern continued during the year, 34, 42 and 113 Squadrons converting from Blenheims and 5 Squadron from Mohawks by the end of 1943; but at that time the first Spitfire Vs appeared in the area, and 136, 607 and 615 Squadrons relinquished their Hurricanes to fly these.

In the United Kingdom the formation of the 2nd Tactical Air Force led to a number of new ground attack squadrons being formed on Hurricane fighter-bombers pending the availability of Typhoons, and during the year 3, 137, 164, 174, 175, 181, 182, 183, 186, 245, 247 and 438 Squadrons flew these aircraft. No. 184 Squadron made the first rocket attack on enemy shipping on 29 July, and 137 and 164 joined in these activities during the year. By January, however, virtually all had converted or were converting to Typhoons.

In the Mediterranean, 6 Squadron soldiered on, joined during 1944 by two Yugoslav squadrons, 351 and 352, though the latter was to convert to Spitfires in June after two months on Hurricanes. Of the other remaining

Above: Mk. I's of No. 306 "Torunski" (Polish) Squadron at readiness sometime during 1941. Note the squadron insignia on nose, PAF insignia on fuselage and red/white fin flash. (IWM)

Above: Starboard side view of UZ-V, V7118 taken at about the same time. (IWM)

Above: UZ-U, V6586 in similar scheme and markings to V above. (IWM)

Below: Good three-quarter front view of UZ-F, K4101 note the underwing roundel and half fuselage to tail and tail-plane in black. F is the centre Hurricane in the top photograph, note the slim presentation of UZ aft of the fuselage roundel. (IWM)

Hurricane units, 94, 213 and 335 Squadrons all received Spifires by the early summer. In England, 309 (Polish) Squadron exchanged its Mustang Is for Hurricanes in April 1944, remaining on defensive duties until October when it converted to Mustang IIIs—the last operational Hurricane unit in Western Europe.

Only in Burma did the Hurricane continue to serve in strength; during 1943-4 units of the Royal Indian Air Force, including 1, 2, 3, 4, 6, 7, 9 and 10 (I.A.F.) Squadrons, had received Hurricanes, and these joined the R.A.F. units in the fighting during the Arakan and Imphal campaigns; eventually about 300 aircraft were supplied to the Indians. Even in the East, however, the Hurricane's days were numbered; in May, 135 Squadron became the first unit to convert to the powerful Republic P-47D Thunderbolt, and it was followed by 146, 261, 30, 134, 258, 79 and 5 Squadrons in that order, before the end of the year, while 17 and 67 Squadrons converted to Spitfire VIIIs.

Most versions of the Hurricane fought in Burma, mainly in a ground strafing rôle. During the second Arakan campaign 20 Squadron operated some Mark IIDs, and later both this squadron and No. 60 received some Mark IVs. During 1945 34, 113, 60 and 42 Squadrons also received Thunderbolts, and 11 Squadron, Spitfires, so that by the end of the war with Japan in August 1945 only 20 Squadron and the Indian units were still operational on the Hurricane.

In the Mediterranean the end of the fighting in May had found 6 and 351 Squadrons still Hurricane-equipped, and while the latter unit transferred to the re-formed Yugoslav Air Force in June, the former retained its aircraft until 1946—the last Hurricane squadron in the R.A.F.

Other than the operational units already mentioned, the Hurricane also served from 1941-1943 with 128 Squadron for the defence of West Africa, and for a year 1423 Flight formed the fighter defence of Iceland, until this was taken over by the Americans in summer 1941. Hurricanes also served with eight "Turbinlite" night-fighter squadrons co-operating with Havocs during 1941/2, with photographic-reconnaissance units in the Middle East, and with many non-operational, experimental and training units throughout the war. In Canada the R.C.A.F.'s 125, 126, 127, 129 and 130 Squadrons flew Hurricanes for several years on home defence duties.

The Sea Hurricane

Mention has already been made of the use of ex-R.A.F. Hurricanes by F.A.A. units from land bases; the first Sea Hurricane IA appeared in 1941, being a navalised Hurricane I, 50 of which were supplied by Fighter Command and 50 more from Canadian production. These were fitted with catapult spools and were mounted on Fighter Catapult Ships from which they were flown by Naval personnel; ten launches were made between June and October 1941 while escorting Atlantic convoys and one Fw 200 was destroyed, two more damaged and others driven away. The place of these was then taken by Catapult Aircraft Merchant Ships, from which the fighters were flown by R.A.F. personnel, and between November 1941 and July 1943—when they ceased operating—six German aircraft were shot down and two damaged. Although it was impossible to recover the aircraft after launching, in all these operations only two pilots were lost.

Meanwhile the first Sea Hurricane with an arrester hook, the Mark IB, had been produced, and this entered service in 1941, the first combat being recorded by 880 Squadron during July. The Mark IB was followed by the IC which mounted four 20 mm. cannons, but reached a maximum speed of only 295 m.p.h. at 15,000 feet, and the first of these joined 811 Squadron in January 1942. The first Sea Hurricane to carry full F.A.A. equipment was the Mark II, joined by the similar Mark XIIA from Canadian production, and this was the main production variant. Added to these were 185 navalised Hurricane IIBs and Cs, but these were not true Sea Hurricanes and were known as Hooked Hurricane IICs.

No. 880 Squadron on H.M.S. *Indomitable* took part in the Allied invasion of Madagascar in May 1942, where it saw little action, but the first major use of the Sea Hurricane was during a big convoy to Malta in June; during this action Sea Hurricanes of 801 Squadron from H.M.S. *Eagle* claimed six Italian aircraft. Two months later the famous August convoy to Malta was fought

Above: Sqdn.Ldr. R. R. Stanford-Tuck, DSO, DFC, in the cockpit of his Hurricane Mk. I at North Weald in November 1940. Note the flag of Burma under the cockpit with the word BURMA in white script below. The serial of this particular Hurricane was V6864 and should not be confused with another DT-A V6962. (IWM)

Below: Sqdn.Ldr. Stanford-Tuck leading a No. 257 Squadron take-off from Coltishall during the winter of 1940. Sgt. Barnes in DT-O V6873 and Plt.Off. Pniak in DT-G V7137. (IWM)

through, and on this occasion four Sea Hurricane squadrons took part, 800 and 880 on *Indomitable*, 801 on *Eagle* and 885 on *Victorious*. Lt. R. Cork of 880 Squadron, flying a Mark IC, shot down five aircraft on 13th August for a total of six in two days, and other Sea Hurricane pilots claimed 15 more enemy aircraft shot down.

In September other Sea Hurricanes of 802 and 883 Squadrons aboard H.M.S. *Avenger* claimed five victories during convoy PQ 18 to North Russia, for the loss of four Sea Hurricanes, but only one pilot, the convoy under their protection suffering little loss. The Sea Hurricane's last big action was providing cover to Operation "Torch", the North African landings, on 8 November 1942. Two carrier forces covering the landings at Oran and Algiers totalled seven carriers with 14 fighter squadrons aboard; amongst these were 802 and 883 on *Avenger*, 804 and 891 on *Dasher* and 800 on *Biter*, all with Sea Hurricanes. No. 800 Squadron enjoyed the greatest success of any of the F.A.A. units involved, claiming a number of Vichy French Dewoitine 520s shot down for no loss while escorting Albacores on the first mission of the day over Oran. Due, however, to the inexperience of several other squadrons, a large number of Sea Hurricanes were lost or damaged due to crashes while landing on the carriers, forced landings, etc.

Following this engagement the Sea Hurricane rapidly disappeared from first line service as more Seafires and American types became available, although they continued to serve on the Atlantic and North Russia convoy routes for some time. Nos. 895 and 897 Squadrons also flew from U.K. bases, and in April 1943 No. 877 Squadron was formed for the defence of Tanganyika. On 26 May 1944 No. 835 Squadron claimed the last Sea Hurricane victories, two Ju 290s, while on the North Russia run, but it was 824 Squadron which flew the final Sea Hurricane operational sorties from H.M.S. *Striker* before re-equipping with Wildcats during the summer of that year.

The Hurricane in Foreign Service

The first overseas delivery of 12 Hurricane Is went to Yugoslavia in December 1938, while during the early summer of 1939 20 were sent to Belgium, 15 flying over and the rest going by sea. Both these countries negotiated manufacturing licences, Yugoslavia setting up production for 100 further aircraft, 40 from Rogozarski and 60 from the Zmaj plant, while Avions Fairey in Belgium was to build 80, armed with four 12.65 mm. machine guns in place of the eight .303s. Those received from England were to have been modified to carry one 12.65 mm. and one .303 in. gun in each wing, but in the event this modification was not performed.

In August 1939 12 more Hurricanes were sold to Rumania, and in the same month two of an order for 18 from Iran were also delivered, though the rest of the order was not to be fulfilled for several years due to the outbreak of war. During September and October a further 12 were delivered to Turkey, and one had already reached Poland. Nine more were *en route* to this country by sea when it surrendered to the Germans late in September, these then being diverted to the R.A.F. in the Middle East. In February 1940 a further 12 were sent to Yugoslavia to try and strengthen Balkan defences against any Axis moves.

The first foreign Hurricanes to see action were those in Belgium; 15 were put into service with *Groupe* I/2 *Le Chardon* (The Thistle) of the 2ème Regiment, coded H21—H35, based at Schaffen with *Groupe* I/1's Gladiators. Only two of the aircraft to be built by Avions Fairey were completed and these do not appear to have entered service. Well before the German invasion of the Low Countries some of these Hurricanes became involved

Above: A couple of Hurricane Mk. IIa's of No. 71 "Eagle" Squadron doing a low-level beat-up of the tarmac area at Kirton-in-Lindsey in the spring of 1941. Note the black port wing of all aircraft. (IWM)

Above: XR-Z revving up prior to take-off from Kirton-in-Lindsey, Lincs. Black port wing. Mk. IIa. (IWM)

Below: Three Hurricane Mk. I's of No. 56 Squadron taking-off from a forward airfield. (IWM)

in a fight with *Luftwaffe* Bf 110s on 3 March 1940, and three were shot down—H22, 23 and 30. Another was damaged in a forced-landing in April, and in consequence only 11 were in service on 9 May. Early next morning the Germans heavily bombed Schaffen, and nine of the Hurricanes were destroyed in this initial attack. The survivors appear to have suffered the same fate shortly afterwards.

Before this happened, 12 R.A.F. Hurricane Is had been taken out of storage and sold to the Finns during the early spring, following Finland's short but heroic war with Soviet Russia, and 11 of these were flown to Finland by Finnish pilots, one crashing *en route* in Norway. The twelfth was later delivered by sea.

By the beginning of April 1941 the Royal Yugoslav Air Force had 38 Hurricanes on hand, about 20 of the licence-built aircraft having been completed, and of these 18 were with the 51st Fighter Squadron, 2nd Regiment, at Sarajevo, 14 with the 33rd Fighter Squadron and six with the 34th Fighter Squadron (which also had eight IK-2s) with the 4th Regiment at Zagreb. When the Germans invaded on 6 April these, in company with IK-2s and -3s, Bf 109Es and Yugoslav Furies, fought for one week; the Hurricanes operated as interceptors over Zagreb and Bosnia, and in a ground attack rôle. By 13 April they were unable to continue due to the rapid German advance, and were ordered to Greece; but fog prevented most taking off, and they were destroyed on the ground by their crews. One or two reached Greece with other Yugoslav aircraft, but were then destroyed on the ground at Paramythia by German bombs.

In June Finland was once more at war with Russia, and here nine Hurricanes formed one flight of HLeLv 30. These took part in the early fighting but were soon reduced to six in strength. Retained for the defence of Helsinki, these six all survived the war but then quickly disappeared; only one remained on strength in 1945, and this aircraft still survives in Finland to the present day.

Following the short stay of 151 Wing in Russia in autumn 1941, large deliveries of Hurricanes were made to that country; a total of 2,952 were sent, mainly Mark IIBs and Cs, though a few IIDs and some IVs were delivered during 1942. Used both by the Red Air Force and the Red Naval Air Fleet, the Hurricanes were to a large extent utilized for fighter-bomber and night intruder operations. Some were adapted to carry .50 in. guns in place of the .303s, and a few were converted into two-seaters, with a dorsal gun position for rear defence.

In the Far East in mid-February 1942, the R.A.F. handed 12 crated Hurricane IIs to the Dutch East Indies forces in Java, part of a recent shipment of 48 new aircraft. These were assembled and, after a few familiarization flights, moved to Kalidjati to begin operations. Two were lost there on training missions, and a few interceptions were flown, but on 24 one was shot down, one crashed while landing and one was destroyed on the ground. The remaining aircraft, now about seven, were ordered to Ngoro for the defence of Eastern Java, and from here on 1 March they joined with Dutch Brewsters and U.S. P-40s in attacking Japanese invasion ships off the coast, creating considerable havoc. On their return they were spotted landing at the previously undiscovered Ngoro base by the Japanese, and before they could be got back into the air they were strafed by Zeros, all being so badly damaged as to be beyond repair.

The only other country to use the Hurricane in action was France, *Groupe de Chasse* 1 of the Free French forces being formed in the Middle East and receiving Hurricanes in January 1942. This unit fought in the Western Desert alongside the R.A.F. until September 1942, when the personnel were transferred to Britain to form 341 Spitfire Squadron. After the Allied invasion of French North Africa, GC II/3 and III/3 of the *Armée de l'Air* converted to Hurricane IIs from Dewoitine 520s during 1942, operating these aircraft on convoy patrols and for training until replaced by P-47s early in 1944.

Also during 1942 14 Mark IIBs and Cs were delivered to Turkey to supplement the earlier Mark Is, and in 1943 ten IICs went to Iran, these being ex-74 Squadron aircraft. The Royal Egyptian Air Force had received some Hurricane Is in 1941, and although these were scrambled whenever Axis raids approached Cairo they undertook no actual operational missions. About 20 Mark IIBs and Cs were later handed over and two squadrons were operational by 1944, No. 1 (Fighter-Reconnaissance) with Mark Is and No. 2 (Fighter) with Mark IICs. At the end of the war 16 more Hurricane IICs were sent to Iran to complete the 1939 contract, and these were used as fighter-trainers, a lone two-seater version also being delivered later.

Early in 1942 one Hurricane I force-landed in Eire, and was purchased by the government of that country for the Irish Air Corps. Two others subsequently force-landed, but these were exchanged for three earlier Mark Is, and other Hurricanes were sold to Eire up to the end of the war, by which time 12 Mark Is and six Mark IICs were in service at Newtownards and Long Kesh, remaining with the Air Corps until 1947.

In 1943, in return for bases in the Azores, the British Government undertook to deliver a quantity of aircraft to Portugal for service in that country's Air Arm. Fifteen Hurricane IICs were initially delivered in August, followed by 50 more IIBs and Cs by the end of the year; these formed the equipment of three new units, *Esquadrilhas* TY, SU and VX, first at Ota Aerial Base and then at Aerial Base No. 3 at Tancos. Fifty more were delivered in 1945, serving at both these airfields and in the Defence of Lisbon Fighter Squadron, and remaining in service until 1951.

The following list covers all known operational squadrons using Hawker Hurricanes from 1938 to 1946. Changes in code letters or area of operation are shown by two separate lines.

The following abbreviations apply:

Duty:	F	Fighter and Fighter-bomber
	FR	Fighter or Tactical-Reconnaissance
	PR	Photographic-Reconnaissance
Base:	UK	United Kingdom
	ME	Mediterranean, including Italy
	FE	India, Burma, Singapore, Ceylon

Royal Air Force Squadrons

Sqn.	Duty	Base	Year	Code	Versions
1	F	UK	38–42	JX	I, IIA, IIB, IIC
3	F	UK	38–43	QO	I, IIB, IIC
5	F	FE	43–44	—	IIC, IID
6	F	ME	41–47	JV	I, IIC, IID, IV
11	F	FE	43–45	—	IIC
17	F	UK	39–41	YB	I, IIA, IIB
		FE	41–44	YB	IIA, IIB, IIC
20	F	FE	43–45	—	IIC, IID
30	F	ME	41–42	RS	I, IIB
		FE	42–44	RS	IIB, IIC
32	F	UK	38–39	KT	I
			39–42	GZ	I, IIB, IIC
		ME	42–43	GZ	IIC
33	F	ME	40–43	NW	I, IIB, IIC
34	F	FE	43–45	—	IIC
42	F	FE	43–45	AW	IIC, IV
43	F	UK	38–42	FT	I, IIB, IIC
		ME	42–43	FT	IIC
46	F	UK	39–39	RJ	I
			39–41	PO	I
		ME	41–41	PO	I
56	F	UK	38–39	LR	I
			39–42	US	I, IIB
60	F	FE	43–45	MU	IIC
67	F	FE	42–44	RD	IIB, IIC
71	F	UK	40–41	XR	I, IIA
73	F	UK	38–39	HV	I
			39–40	TP	I
		ME	40–43	TP	I, IIB, IIC
74	F	ME	42–43	ZP	IIB
79	F	UK	38–39	AL	I
			39–42	NV	I, IIB
		FE	42–44	NV	IIB, IIC
80	F	ME	40–43	AP	I, IIA, IIB
81	F	UK*	41–41	FE	IIB
85	F	UK	38–39	NO	I
			39–41	VY	I
87	F	UK	38–39	PD	I
			39–42	LK	I, IIC
		ME	42–44	LK	IIC

Sqn.	Duty	Base	Year	Code	Versions
94	F	ME	41–42	GO	I, IIB
			42–44	GO	IIC
111	F	UK	37–39	TM	I
			39–41	JU	I
113	F	FE	43–45	AD	IIC
121	F	UK	41–41	AV	I, IIB
123	F	ME	42–44	XE	IIC
126	F	ME	41–42	—	IIA, IIB
127	F	ME	41–14	—	I
			42–43	BZ	I, IIB, IIC
128	F	ME	41–43	WG	I, IIB
133	F	UK	41–41	MD	IIB
134	F	UK*	41–41	GV	IIB
		ME	43–43	GQ	IIB, IIC
		FE	44–44	GQ	IIC
135	F	UK	41–41	WK	IIA
		FE	42–44	WK	IIB, IIC
136	F	UK	41–41	HM	IIA, IIB
		FE	42–43	HM	IIB, IIC
137	F	UK	43–44	SF	IV
145	F	UK	40–41	SO	I
146	F	FE	42–44	—	IIB, IIC
151	F	UK	38–39	GG	I
			39–41	DZ	I
164	F	UK	43–44	FJ	IV
174	F	UK	42–43	XP	IIB
175	F	UK	42–43	HH	IIB
176	F	FE	43–44	—	IIC
181	F	UK	42–43	EL	I
182	F	UK	42–43	XM	I
183	F	UK	42–43	HF	I
184	F	UK	42–44	BR	IID, IV
185	F	ME	41–42	—	I, IIA, IIC
186	F	UK	43–43	AP	IV
208	FR	ME	40–42	—	I, II
213	F	UK	39–41	AK	I
		ME	41–44	AK	I, IIC

*Squadrons so marked also operated in North Russia in 1941

225	FR	UK	40–42	—	I, II
		ME	42–43	—	II
229	F	UK	40–41	RE	I
		ME	41–42	HB	I, IIC
232	F	UK	40–42	EF	I, IIB
237	FR	ME	41–41	—	I
	F	ME	42–43	DV	I, IIC
238	F	UK	40–41	VK	I
		ME	41–43	RS	I, IIA, IIB, IIC
239	FR	UK	41–43	HB	
241	FR	ME	42–43		II
242	F	UK	40–41	LE	I, IIB, IIC
		ME	41–42	LE	IIB
		FE	42–42	—	IIB
245	F	UK	40–41	DX	I, IIB
			41–43	MR	IIB, IIC
247	F	UK	40–41	HP	I, IIA
			41–43	ZY	IIA, IIB, IIC
249	F	UK	40–41	GN	I, IIA
		ME	41–42	—	I, IIA, IIB, IIC
250	F	ME	42–42	LD	I, IIC
253	F	UK	40–42	SW	I, IIB, IIC, IIA
		ME	42–43	SW	IIC
255	F	UK	41–41	YD	I
257	F	UK	40–41	DT	I, IIB, IIC
			41–42	FM	I, IIA, IIB, IIC
258	F	UK	40–41	ZT	I, IIA
		FE	42–42	—	IIA
		FE	42–44	ZT	I, IIB, IIC
260	F	UK	40–41	HS	I
		ME	41–42	HS	I
261	F	ME	40–42	—	I, IIB
		FE	42–44	FJ	IIB, IIC
263	F	UK	40–40	HE	I
273	F	FE	42–44	VY	I, IIA, IIB, IIC
274	F	ME	40–43	YK	I, IIB, IIC
302	F	UK	40–41	WX	I, IIA, IIB
303	F	UK	40–41	RF	I
306	F	UK	40–41	UZ	I, IIA
308	F	UK	40–41	ZF	I
309	F	UK	44–44	WC	IIC
310	F	UK	40–41	NN	I, IIA, IIB
312	F	UK	40–41	DU	I, IIB
315	F	UK	41–41	PK	I
316	F	UK	41–41	SZ	I, IIA, IIB
317	F	UK	41–41	JH	I, IIA IIB
331	F	UK	41–41	FN	I, IIB
335	F	ME	41–44	FG	I, IIB, IIC
336	F	ME	43–44		IIC
351	F	ME	44–45	—	IIC, IV

Sqn.	Duty	Base	Year	Code	Versions
352	F	ME	44–44	—	IIC
401	F	UK	40–41	YO	I, IIB
402	F	UK	40–42	AE	I, IIA, IIB
417	F	ME	42–43	AN	IIB, IIC
438	F	UK	43–44	F3	IV
439	F	UK	44–44	5V	IV
440	F	UK	44–44	I8	IV
451	FR	ME	41–43	—	I, IIC
486	F	UK	42–42	SA	IIB
488	F	FE	42–42	—	I
501	F	UK	39–39	ZH	I
			39–41	SD	I
504	F	UK	39–41	TM	I, IIB
531	F	UK	41–43	—	IIC
532	F	UK	41–43	—	IIC
533	F	UK	41–43	—	IIC
534	F	UK	41–43	—	IIC
537	F	UK	41–43	—	IIC
538	F	UK	41–43	—	IIC
601	F	UK	40–41	UF	I, IIB
605	F	UK	39–41	UP	I, IIA, IIB
		ME	41–42	—	IIB
		FE	42–42	—	IIB
607	F	UK	40–42	AF	I, IIA, IIB
		FE	42–43	AF	IIB, IIC
615	F	UK	40–42	KW	I, IIA, IIB, IIC
		FE	42–43	KW	IIB, IIC
3RAAF	F	ME	41–41	CV	I
1SAAF	F	ME	40–42	AX	I, IIA, IIB, IIC
2SAAF	F	ME	40–41	—	I
3SAAF	F	ME	40–44	CA	I, IIB, IIC
7SAAF	F	ME	42–43		I, IIB, IID, IIC
40SAAF	FR	ME	42–43		II
41SAAF		ME			
680 (ex 2 PRU)					
681 (ex 3 PRU)					

Non-operational use of the Hurricane by the following squadrons:—267, 279, 283, 285, 286, 288, 289, 290, 421, 422, 514, 516, 521, 527, 567, 577, 587, 595 631, 639, 667, 650, 695.

The following Flights also operated Hurricanes: 1413(Met), 1414(Met) 1415(Met), 1423(Defence of Iceland, 1941), 1435(Night Fighter Malta, 1941)

Sqn.	Duty	Base	Year	Versions
Royal Indian Air Force				
1	F	FE	42–45	II
2	F	FE	42–45	II
3	F	FE	43–45	II
4	F	FE	43–45	II
6	F	FE	42–45	II
7	F	FE	44–45	II
9	F	FE	43–45	II
10	F	FE	44–45	II
Royal Canadian Air Force (home based only)				
125	F	Can		
126	F	Can		
127	F	Can		
129	F	Can		
130	F	Can		
Fleet Air Arm (Sea Hurricanes, except where noted to the contrary)				
800	F	UK & ME	42–43	I, II
801	F	UK & ME	41–42	
802	F	UK & ME	42–42	
803	F	ME	41–41	Hurricanes only (ex-RAF)
804	F	UK & ME	41–43	
805	F	ME	41–41	Hurricanes only (ex-RAF)
806	F	ME	41–41	Hurricanes only (ex-RAF)
811	F	UK	41–41	Non-operational
824	F	UK	43–44	
825	F	UK	43–44	
835	F	UK	43–44	
877	F	ME	43–44	Hurricanes only (ex-RAF)
880	F	UK, FE & ME	41–42	
883	F	UK & ME	41–42	
885	F	UK & ME	41–42	
889	F	ME	42–43	Hurricanes only (ex-RAF)
891	F	UK & ME	42–43	
895	F	UK	42–43	Non-operational
897	F	UK	42–43	Non-operational

In the case of FAA squadrons, UK includes the Atlantic and North Russia areas.

Above & below: Hurricane IIa's of No. 1423 Flight on Kaldanes airfield, Iceland in early 1941. Note the non-standard leading edge join of upper and under surface camouflage. No. 1423 Flight was formed from No. 98 Bomber Squadron. (IWM)

Left: A Mk. IIb of No. 134 Squadron, No. 151 Wing operating from Vaenga airfield near Archangel in North Russia during the winter of 1941. The letter code was for the benefit of RAF ground crews, the numerals for Russian ground crews. Serial is Z5253. (IWM)

Below: Hurricane IIb of No. 81 Squadron on the airfield at Vaenga in the autumn of 1941, serial Z5227. The letters are in grey, the numerals in white. (IWM)

Above: Good detail shot of a Mk. IIb of No. 81 Squadron, serial Z3768, FK-49 in grey. (IWM)

Right: Hurricane IIb's of No. 81 Squadron at Vaenga, top Z3977 FN in grey, 55 in white; below Z4018 FH in; grey, 41 in white, standard RAF camouflage. (IWM)

Below: A IIb of No. 134 Squadron being serviced by a Russian ground crew during the 1941 winter. Serial Z3203 GG in grey, 20 in white. (IWM)

Fine flying shots of two Hurricane Mk. IIb's of No. 402 Squadron, top BE492, above: AE-W BE495. (via Francis K. Mason)

Below: BE417, another Mk. IIb of No. 402 Squadron being bombed-up at Rochford, armament comprised 12 x ·303 machine guns and 2 x 250lb bombs. No. 402 was the second Hurribomber squadron to go on cross-channel ops., commencing in November 1941. (via Francis K. Mason)

Two good photographs of an old Hurricane Mk. I in a very interesting paint scheme. The aircraft is believed to be P2798 which saw service with the squadron in France during 1939–40 and subsequently in the night-fighter role in the UK. See colour illustration. (IWM)

Right: A Mk. IIc of No. 87 Squadron being serviced and re-armed with 20mm ammunition. (Charles E. Brown)

Below: "Nightingale", a Mk. IIc night-fighter of No. 87 Squadron at Charmy Down in September 1942. Serial is HL864 in small letters directly beneath the tail-plane. (IWM)

Above: A Canadian built Hurricane Mk. X of Fighter Leaders School, FLS. (IWM)

Above: A good flying shot of another Canadian built Mk. X of No. 55 Operational Training Unit, OTU. Note the full span yellow leading edge, serial is AG162. (IWM)

Below: An early Hurricane Mk. IIc of No. 3 Squadron, BD867 QO-Y. This squadron was engaged in offensive daylight sweeps during 1941. (via Francis K. Mason)

Above: Neat and tidy formation by Mk. IIc's of No. 3 Squadron during 1941. Serials Z Z3464; P BD869; F Z3069; T Z3092; R Z3094 and Y BD867. (IWM)

Excellent flying shots of Hurricane Mk. IIc night-fighters of No. 247 Squadron, 1942. Above; ZY-S BD936 and below in company with ZY-V BE638 note the position of the serial on top of the fuselage just ahead of the fin, serials and codes in red. (IWM)

Above: An anti-tank Hurricane Mk. IId of No. 164 Squadron at Middle Wallop in June 1943 shortly before becoming operational on anti-shipping sweeps over the English Channel. (via Francis K. Mason)

Below: Fine plan view detail shot of an anti-tank Mk. IV. (Charles E. Brown)

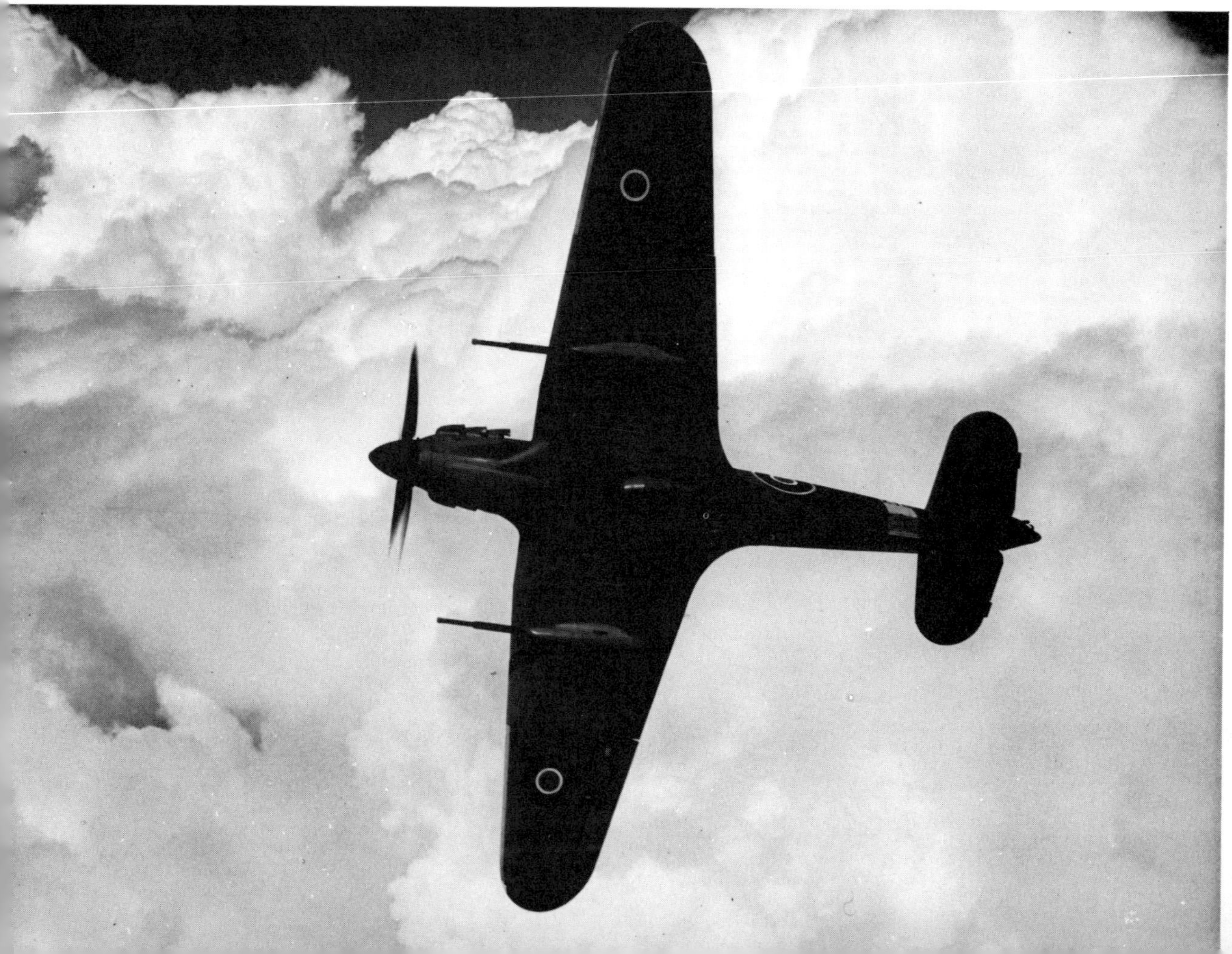

Above: Neat formation of early Hurricane Mk. I's flying over Egypt in late 1940. No doubt these aircraft had been crated out to West Africa and assembled there hence the chalked serial on the wing and rudder of T9530 the nearest aircraft. The route to Egypt was across Central Africa to Khartoum in the Sudan, usually in formations of nine with a Blenheim Mk. IV navigating. Note absence of tropical filters. (IWM)

Above: An early tropicalised Mk. I over the desert, black port wing with roundel, white starboard with roundel painted out, fairly common during 1941. Serial PZ627. (IWM)

Below: An early Hurricane Mk. I firing its guns in Beau Geste style butts at an MU in Egypt, 1941. (IWM)

Above: Hurricane Mk. I's of No. 1 Squadron, South African Air Force, flying past Jebel Kassala on the Sudan-Eritrean frontier, typical of the rugged, inhospitable country along the length of the Sudanese frontier with Eritrea and Abyssinia. Kassala landing ground is just to the left out of the picture. (IWM)

Above & below: A pair of Mk. I's of No. 1 SAAF on Agordat landing ground, Eritrea, in early 1941.

Above. Line-up of Hurricane Mk. I's and II's of No. 213 Squadron on Famagusta airfield, Cyprus, Nov. 1941. Note only two aircraft have tropical filters. Nearest aircraft is F W9349. (IWM)

Below: A Mk. I of No. 213 Squadron being re-armed on Famagusta airfield. (IWM)

Above, left: A No. 213 formation over Cyprus. Right, interesting adaptation of the roundel on a No. 213 aircraft. (photos G. H. Westlake via C. F. Shores)

Below: Hurricane Mk. IIc of No. 213 Squadron on El Alamein landing ground, Western Desert in late 1942. Serial HL887. Note the inboard pair of 20mm cannon have been removed; at this time the squadron was engaged on long-range escort duties. (IWM).

Above: Five Hurricanes taking-off from a typical desert landing ground. (IWM)

Above: A pair of Mk. I's of No. 237 "Rhodesian" Squadron taking-off from a desert landing ground during 1942. (IWM)

Below: Typical desert take-off with everyone trying to keep out of everyone else's dust. (IWM)

A

Mk. I, No. 56 Squadron, RAF, North Weald. 1938.

2
Mk. I, No. 85 Squadron, RAF, Debden, 1939.

3
Mk. I, No. 85 Squadron, RAF, Debden, 1939.

4
Mk. I, No. 85 Squadron, RAF, Merville, France, May 1940.

5
Mk. I, No. 85 Squadron, RAF, Kirton-in-Lindsey, Battle of Britain, November 1940.

6
Mk. I, No. 85 Squadron, RAF, Gravesend. Battle of Britain, November 1940.

1
Mk. I, No. 111 Squadron, RAF, Northolt, 1938.

2
Mk. I, No. 73 Squadron, RAF, No. 67 Wing, Advanced Air Striking Force, RAF, Rouves, France, 1940.

3
Mk. I, No. 17 Squadron, RAF, Debden, Battle of Britain, September 1940.

4
Mk. I, No. 145 Squadron, RAF, West Hampnett, Battle of Britain July 1940.

5
Mk. I, No. 151 Squadron, RAF, North Weald, August 1939.

6
Mk. I, No. 151 Squadron, RAF, Martlesham Heath, May 1940.

©WARD

c

k. I, No. 303 (Polish) Squadron, RAF, Northolt, Battle of
ritain, August–October 1940.

k. I, No. 306 (Polish) Squadron, RAF, Kirton-in-Lindsey,
arly 1942.

k. IIb, No. 81 Squadron, No. 151 Wing, RAF, Vaenga, Nr.
rchangel, North Russia, 1941.

Ik. IIa, No. 71 "Eagle" Squadron, RAF, Kirton-in-Lindsey,
arly 1941.

Ik. I, No. 527 (Calibration) Squadron, RAF, Hornchurch, 1943.

Mk.I, Central Flying School, RAF, Uphaven, 1940. Gunnery Flight.

©WARD

D

1
Mk. I, No. 312 (Czechoslovak) Squadron, RAF, Speke, 1941.

2
Mk. I, No. 87 Squadron, RAF, 1940.

3
Mk. IIc, No. 87 Squadron, RAF, Charmy Down, 1942.

4
Mk. X (Canadian built), Fighter Leaders School, RAF.

5
Mk. IId, No. 164 Squadron, RAF, Middle Wallop, June 1943.

6
Mk. IIc, No. 83 Operational Training Unit, Gunnery Flight, RAF, Peplow, 1944.

E

1
Mk. IIB, No. 73 Squadron, Desert Air Force, RAF, Western Desert, 1941-2.

2
PR Mk. I, No. 208 (Army Co-operation) Squadron, Desert Air Force, RAF, Burg el Arab, Egypt, 1942.

3
Mk. IIc, No. 213 Squadron, Desert Air Force, RAF, El Alamein Egypt, 1942.

4
Mk. IId. No. 6 Squadron, Desert Air Force, RAF, Shandur/Sidi Heneish, Egypt, 1942.

5
Mk. IIb, No. 128 Squadron, RAF, Hastings, Sierra Leone, West Africa, 1942-3.

6
Mk. IIc, No. 30 Squadron, RAF, Ratmanala, Ceylon, 1942.

F

1
Mk. IV, No. 6 Squadron, Desert Air Force, RAF, Prkos, Yugoslavia, May 1945.

2
PR Mk. IIc, No. 208 (Army Co-operation) Squadron, Desert Air Force, RAF, El Bassa, Palestine, 1943.

3
Mk. IIc, No. 34 Squadron, RAF, Burma, 1944.

4
Mk. I, Merchant Service Fighter Unit, RAF, Catapult Armed Merchant Ship "Empire Tide", 1942.

5
Sea Hurricane Mk. XII (Canadian built) Fleet Air Arm, St. Leu, Algiers, Operation Torch, 1944.

6
Mk. IIc, No. 1 Squadron, Indian Air Force, Imphal, Assam, 1944.

1
Mk. I, 2nd Squadron, 1st Group, 2nd Regiment, Belgian Air Force, Schaffen 1940.

2
Mk. IIc, Turkish Air Force, 1942.

3
Mk. I, HLeLv 30, Finnish Air Force, 1941.

4
Mk. I, HLeLv 30, Finnish Air Force 1942.

5
Mk. IIc, 72nd Regiment, Red Naval Air Fleet, Vaenga, Nr. Archangel, North Russia, 1942.

6
Mk. IIb, Russian Air Force, 1942.

1
Mk. IIc, Irish Air Corps, Baldonnel, 1945.

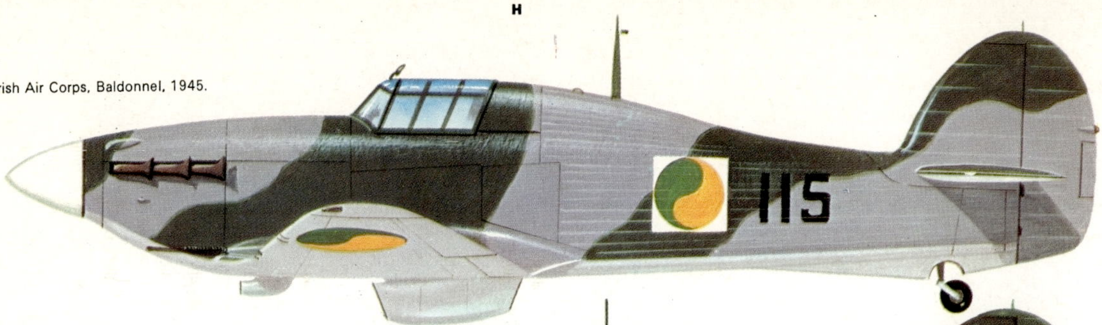

2
Mk. I, Yugoslav Air Force, 1940.

3
Mk. IV No. 351 (Yugoslav) Squadron, RAF, Prkos, Yugoslavia, 1944-5.

4
Mk. IIc, Lisbon Defence Flight, Portuguese Air Force, 1948.

5
Mk. IIc, Advanced Group, Flying Training School, Persian Air Force, Doshan Teppeh, 1946.

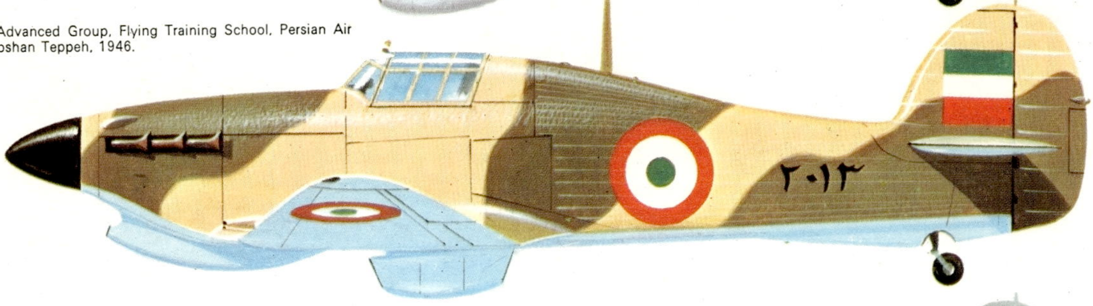

6
T Mk. IIc, Persian Air Force, 1947.

Above: A pair of Mk. IIc's in the markings of No. 94 Squadron formating with three replacement aircraft over the Delta area, Egypt. All aircraft with azure blue under surfaces, note the exhaust scorch mark has been painted in on G. (IWM)

Below: HL844, farthest aircraft in the above formation and one of the three Hurricanes presented by Lady MacRobert in memory of her three sons, all of whom lost their lives flying during the War. (IWM)

Below: A formation of Hurricane IId's of No. 6 Squadron over the Western Desert sometime in 1942. No. 6 was the first of the 2 x 40mm tank-busters and went operational for the first time in June 1942. (IWM)

Above: Hurricane Mk. IV of No. 6 Squadron coming in to land at Tatoi, Greece late in 1944. Serial is LF498. (IWM)

Above: A Mk. IV with typical load of rockets and long-range tank taking-off from a Balkan airfield. (IWM)

Below: Mk. IV's of No. 6 Squadron dispersed on Prkos airfield, Yugoslavia in May 1944. (IWM)

A Mk. IIb of No. 73 Squadron, damaged during action over the desert being loaded on a "queen mary" for return to a MU in the Delta area. Note the squadron marking an adaptation of No. 73's yellow and blue flash of pre-war days. Originally the marking was blue and yellow on the Hurricanes but this was changed to an overall blue flash with two thin yellow lines as shown in the photograph; the marking was subsequently applied on the squadron's Spitfire Mk. IX's. (IWM)

Hurricane PR Mk. I of No. 208 (Army Co-operation) Squadron. Note the squadron marking on the fuselage and the "sand and spaghetti" nose scheme, see colour illustration. This particular aircraft was shot down by Bf.109F's near Burg el Arab on 24 July 1942. (IWM)

Another PR Mk. I of 208 Squadron showing the "sand and spaghetti" scheme applied to the nose and leading edge of the wings. (via Francis K. Mason)

Hurricane PR Mk. II of No. 208 Squadron photographed at Kabrit, Egypt in 1942. Note the ventral camera housing aft of the radiator, Serial DG630 (previously a Mk. I V6535), the scheme is the same as HL830, see colour illustration.

Hurricane Mk. I, one of the few aircraft abandoned to the Germans in the desert during the retreat of March 1941, subsequently recaptured by the 8th Army on Gambut landing ground. (IWM)

Two shots showing variations of the black and white undersides, a third scheme was geometrically divided down the centre-line. The above photo was taken over Cyprus, that below over Crete in early 1941. (IWM)

Above: A Mk. I being put through its paces over the desert, note the full span yellow leading edge. (IWM)

Above: Detail shots of IIc and IId armament, to the left the 40mm cannons of the IId and right the 20mm Hispanos of the IIc; this particular aircraft is HL851 and carried the code O-P, see photo of 94 Squadron formation. (IWM)

Below: Hurricane Mk. IIb of No. 128 Squadron flying over West Africa; the squadron defended the ports and bases of Sierra Leone from October 1941 to March 1943. See colour illustration. (IWM)

Above: A pair of Hurricane Mk. IId's, believed to be from No. 20 Squadron, searching out targets along the Arakan coast. (IWM)

Above: Bombed up Mk. IIc preparing to take-off from a Burmese airfield. (IWM)
Below: A Hurricane Mk. IV flying low over the Irrawaddy River by the Aya Bridge near Mandalay early in 1945. (IWM).

Left: A Hurricane Mk. IIc of No. 34 Squadron on a Burmese airfield sometime during 1944. Serial is LB935. Standard green grey camouflage. (IWM)

Above: An unarmed Mk. IIc, BM565, one of many Hurricanes relegated to training duties towards the end of the war. This particular aircraft shown here flying over Bengal served with GATU until 1947. The scheme is overall matt black, roundels are standard red, white and blue. (IWM)

Below: An Indian Air Force Mk. I running up its Merlin III before taking-off on a training flight. (IWM)

Above: Formation of early Sea Hurricane Ib's of the Fleet Air Arm. (IWM)

Right: Sea Hurricane Ib displaying arrester hook, unit unknown. (IWM)

Below: Sea Hurricane Ib being serviced on a light carrier, note the cut-out for the arrester hook. (IWM)

Above: Interesting shot of a Sea Hurricane immediately after take-off from a light carrier. (IWM)

Left: A pair of Sea Hurricanes of the Fleet Air Arm camouflaged with US insignia forced landed on the beach at St. Leu, Nr. Algiers on 8 November 1942 shortly after the Torch landings. Top a 12 x ·303 gun Canadian built Sea Hurricane Mk. XII and below a 4 x 20mm cannon Canadian Sea Hurricane Mk. X, serials respectively are JS327 and AM277. See colour illustration. (via R. Ward)

Left: A Sea Hurricane Mk. Ia with partial flap selected is discharged from a rocket catapult at the Catapult Training Unit at Speke in 1941. (IWM)

Hurricane Mk. I of the Merchant Service Fighter Unit on board the Catapult Armed Merchant (CAM) Ship *Empire Tide*. Top photo shows V6756 on its catapult, middle a trial launch and below a starboard view on the catapult. (IWM)

Hurricane Mk. I of the 2nd Squadron, 1st Group, 2nd Regiment, Belgian Air Force, probably at Schaffen during the winter of 1939. White 21 on rudder, black H 21 on undersurfaces of wings, standard RAF camouflage. (Lt.-Col. M. C. Terlinden)

A couple of shots of Hurricane Mk. I, 22, probably taken in 1939 shortly after delivery, H22 on under surfaces of wings. (Lt.-Col. M. C. Terlinden)

Belgian Hurricane Mk. I with Rotol propeller. (Lt.-Col. M. C. Terlinden)

No. 27 complete with "Thistle" insignia of the 2nd Squadron. (Lt.-Col. M. C. Terlinden)

Above: A couple of Hurricanes of the crack fighter squadron on their noses in soft ground at Wevelghem! Note 25 carries the "Thistle" but 24 does not; the code H-25 is clearly shown on the under surfaces. (Lt.-Col. M. C. Terlinden)

Below left & right: Line-up of Hurricanes of the 2nd Squadron at Schaffen in 1940. (Lt.-Col. M. C. Terlinden)

Below: A very interesting photograph of a RAF Hurricane Mk. I of No. 87 Squadron, AASF, which made a forced landing on the road between Courtrai and Moucron, the aircraft was repaired by the Belgians and put back in commission with the number 45 in BAF markings at Schaffen and destroyed on the tarmac during the first German assault. (Lt.-Col. M. C. Terlinden).

Above: Hurricane Mk. I's of HLeLv 30 of the Finnish Air Force in early 1941 still in RAF camouflage, HC458 without underwing insignia, Hurricane in distance with. (E. Ritaranta)

Above: HU460, a Hurricane Mk. I of HLeLv 30 in RAF camouflage, note this aircraft has underwing insignia. (via Francis K. Mason)

Above & below: Hurricane Mk. I of HLeLv 30 in early 1942 after repainting in standard Finnish Air Force camouflage and Continuation War markings. (E. Ritaranta)

Russian Hurricane in standard RAF camouflage, red star with white outline on upper surfaces, without on under surfaces, white 18 on fuselage. (IWM)

Hurricane Mk. IIb of the 72nd Regiment of the Red Naval Air Fleet at Vaenga in North Russia, an ex No. 151 Wing aircraft. Note the armament only comprises eight guns and that the RAF roundel is faintly discernable on the under surface of the wing. (IWM)

A Hurricane in rare markings, a French Naval Hurricane exhibited shortly after the War near the Arc de Triomphe in Paris, probably one left behind by the RAF in North Africa. (G. J. R. Skillen)

A Hurricane Mk. IIc of the Turkish Air Force at an RAF MU in the Middle East sometime during 1942. (IWM)

Hurricane Mk. IIc of the Portuguese Air Force at Langley before delivery in 1945. (Hawker)

Above: Fine flying shot of a Hurricane Mk. I of the Yugoslav Air Force, standard RAF camouflage. (Hawker)

Above: Hurricane Mk. IV's of No. 351 (Yugoslav) Squadron armed with rockets on Prkos airfield, Yugoslavia during 1944. (IWM)

Left: Hurricane Mk. IV of the Yugoslav Air Force, overall grey scheme, serial 9539 in black on fin.

Hurricane Mk. IIc in standard RAF desert camouflage, of the Persian Air Force, used as fighter trainers by the Advanced Group of the Persian FTS at Doshan Teppeh. (Hawker)

Two-seat Hurricane Mk. IIc trainer of the Persian Air Force.

Below: Good flying shot of a Persian two-seater with early open cockpits and right, with the addition of a less draughty instructor's seat, a modified Tempest sliding hood. (Hawker)

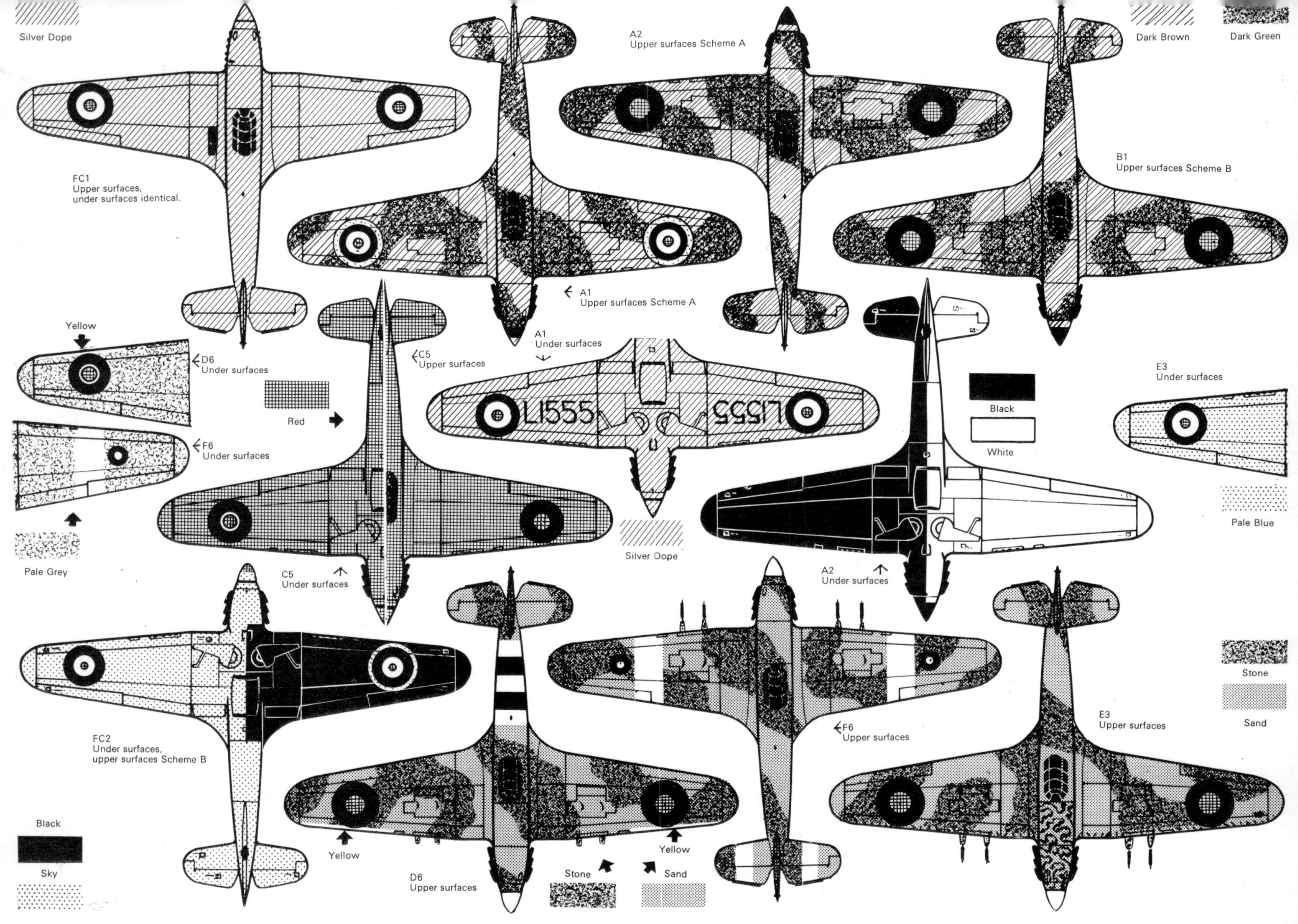

Silver Dope
FC1
Upper surfaces,
under surfaces identical.
A2
Upper surfaces Scheme A
A1
Upper surfaces Scheme A
Dark Brown
Dark Green
B1
Upper surfaces Scheme B
Yellow
D6
Under surfaces
F6
Under surfaces
Pale Grey
Red
C5
Upper surfaces
A1
Under surfaces
L1555
L1555
Silver Dope
C5
Under surfaces
Black
White
A2
Under surfaces
E3
Under surfaces
Pale Blue
FC2
Under surfaces,
upper surfaces Scheme B
Black
Sky
Yellow
Yellow
D6
Upper surfaces
Stone
Sand
F6
Upper surfaces
E3
Upper surfaces
Stone
Sand